Wo

For

Dr. Mindy H. Pelz's

Fast Like a Girl:

A Woman's Guide to Using the Healing Power of Fasting to Burn Fat, Boost Energy, and Balance Hormones

Smart Reads

Note to readers:
This is an unofficial workbook for Dr. Mindy Pelz's "Fast Like a Girl: A Woman's Guide to Using the Healing Power of Fasting to Burn Fat, Boost Energy, and Balance Hormones" designed to enrich your reading experience. The original book can be purchased on Amazon.

Download Your Free Gift

As a way to say "Thank You" for being a fan of our series, I've included a free gift for you:

Brain Health: How to Nurture and Nourish Your Brain For Top Performance

Go to www.smart-reads.com to get your FREE book.

The Smart Reads Team

Table of Contents

Overview of *Fast Like a Girl: A Woman's Guide to Using the Healing Power of Fasting to Burn Fat, Boost Energy, and Balance Hormones*

Fast Like a Girl is Dr. Mindy H. Pelz's most recent book. In this book, the author shares her passion and frustration for fasting. Fasting has a myriad of health benefits. However, due to hormonal differences between men and women, women need to fast differently than men. In this book, the author details her personal experience and research for fasting. Additionally, the author includes stories of women who began to fast according to their hormones instead of trying to fast like a man.

The book begins with a forward from LeAnn Rimes. If this name sounds familiar, LeAnn Rimes is a two-time Grammy-winning singer and songwriter. In the forward, Rimes discusses her personal struggles with health, including inflammation and painful periods. For years, Rimes kept these symptoms in check with hormonal birth control. However, around the pandemic's start, Rimes decided it was time to listen to her body again. On her journey to better health, Rimes discovered Dr. Pelz's book The Menopause Reset. Through following Dr. Pelz's methodology and one-on-one lessons, LeAnn Rimes saw the benefits of listening to your body and fasting like a girl.

LeAnn Rimes ends the forward with a poem for women. This poem serves as a reminder that women have a natural rhythm. Secondly, women should not feel pressured to follow society's ideals but should instead find their own path. Lastly, women should follow Mother Nature and live following their hormonal cycle.

After the forward, the author details her history with fasting. As a student-athlete, the author loved being active. This changed when she was diagnosed with chronic fatigue. The author visited a doctor who provided little help and no solutions. The author's mother, frustrated with the diagnosis, took the author to another doctor.

This next doctor was a holistic medical doctor. He suggested a change to the author's diet. After following this diet, which was very similar to the popular ketogenic diet, the author saw improvements in only three weeks. After seeing the sudden health improvements in her own life, the author wanted to learn more about food's effects on our health.

In the United States, 60% of the population has at least one chronic disease. Another frightening statistic is that only 12% of Americans have good metabolic health. Metabolic health is the body's ability to regulate blood sugar, blood pressure, and cholesterol without the use of medication. Considering so few Americans have good metabolic health and aren't suffering from chronic diseases, a new health tool is needed. The author believes fasting is the way to improve health.

Dr. Pelz has helped her clients implement fasting in their own life and reap the health benefits. However, throughout her career, Dr. Pelz soon found that her patients had three key questions when it came to fasting:

1. How long should a fast be?

2. What should I eat when not fasting?

3. Should women fast differently from men?

To address these questions, the author began writing this book. The author has divided the information into three main parts. In the first part, the author details the hormones that affect women so they can better understand how fasting can support these hormones. This part also discusses the concept of metabolic switching, a process of varying your diet depending on your hormones. This first part of the book encompasses chapters one through four.

In the book's second part, covering chapters five through seven, the author discusses common health goals and how fasting can support these goals. This part of the book also lists specific foods you should avoid and other foods you should add to your diet. The final chapter of this section lays out the fasting cycle, a detailed diet, and a fasting plan tailored to a woman's menstrual cycle.

The final part of the book contains chapters eight through eleven. This section begins with a thirty-day fasting reset. Women with or without a period can use this reset. It is designed to help any woman easily implement fasting in her daily life. This final section also contains information on the best way to end a fast, depending on your health goals. Additionally, the third section has tips to make fasting easier and contains recipes designed for different phases of your menstrual cycle.

Chapter 1: It's Not Your Fault

The first chapter of the book, "It's Not Your Fault," opens with a brief explanation of cells, nutrients, and hormones within the human body. The author notes that there are over thirty-trillion cells in the human body, all working together to keep you alive. Every time you eat, your body takes the nutrients in the food and supplies them to your cells. A receptor surrounds each cell. These receptors can open and close based on hormones in your body, letting hormones into your cells or keeping them out.

The book recognizes that many diets do not consider these cells and hormones. In fact, many diets can damage the cell and hormone's natural processes. The author acknowledges five key dieting mistakes that can do more harm than good when helping you lose weight and supporting your health. These five dieting mistakes are:

1. Diets that restrict calories

2. Diets with low-quality food

3. Diets that do not address cortisol

4. Diets that do not limit toxins

5. Diets that are not tailored to the individual

Diets that restrict calories are the first diet the author recognizes as problematic. The book notes that many people consider counting calories the key to staying thin. But this is not the case. As the author points out, everybody has a certain amount of calories to maintain a constant weight. The particular amount of calories required is called the set point. The author says that when you eat fewer calories, your body eventually gets used to the fewer calories and adjusts your body's set point. This does far more harm than good, as you will have to eat fewer calories to continue seeing weight loss.

The author supports these claims with examples from the Minnesota Starvation Experiment conducted in the 1960s. In this study, 36 men were given drastically reduced caloric intake to study the effects of starvation. After the experiment was completed, the participants reported worsened mental health and a 10% increase in their body weight from before the experiment.

The next harmful diet technique included in this book is poor-quality food. The author notes that low-fat and fat-free foods are common health options. But these choices aren't as healthy as they may seem. The author explains that low-fat and fat-free foods often have added sugars to make the food more palatable. Bodies produce more insulin to process these additional sugars. Too much insulin for too long prevents the body from correctly processing the insulin and sugar. Eventually, the body begins to store insulin and sugar as fat. This process is known as insulin resistance, and it is counterproductive to weight loss.

The third harmful diet issue the author addresses is increased cortisol. Cortisol is a hormone released during times of stress. When cortisol rises, so does insulin. As the author discussed in the previous diet problem, increased insulin can cause many issues. Cortisol can increase from such stressful situations as limiting calories. However, cortisol spikes can occur for reasons unrelated to food, like excessive exercise, workplace problems, or relationship issues. The author notes that women are more susceptible to stress than men. So any healthy diet should address this issue and seek to lower cortisol.

Another harmful diet technique the book addresses are toxins. When toxins are introduced to the body, our cells can store them as fat to protect the body. The author recommends rethinking how one considers fat. It can actually protect us. Some of the worst toxins the book recognizes are BPA plastics, phthalates, atrazine, organotins, and perfluorooctanoic acids (PFOA). However, these are just a few of the toxins our bodies may be exposed to. The author notes that this book will not cover all toxins prevalent in our environment but will focus on toxins in food. The author provides two examples of toxins in food: monosodium glutamate and soy protein isolates. The authors continue with an acknowledgment that more food toxins will be covered in chapter six.

The final counterproductive diet technique addressed in this chapter is not tailoring diets to the individual. For example, the book notes that two hormones women have, estrogen and progesterone, have different needs. Estrogen prefers a low-carb diet, whereas progesterone favors a diet with more carbs. Ultimately, the author notes that any diet should consider women's natural hormonal cycles. Additionally, the author recommends diets should be tailored to each individual.

To close the first chapter, the author ends with a story of Sarah. After fighting against poor health for years, Sarah finally decided to take her health into her own hands. Finding the author's Youtube videos, Sarah began to follow a fasting schedule for her health needs. Following this diet, Sarah lost 80 pounds and astounded her doctors with her improved health.

Key Points

1. Many diets are not designed for women and can do more harm than good.

2. Restricting calories trains your body to need fewer calories, making it harder to lose weight.

3. Low-fat and fat-free foods can lead to insulin resistance due to the added sugars in these foods.

4. When stressed, your body releases cortisol which can impact your ability to lose weight.

5. Your body stores toxins as fat, so removing toxins from your diet is essential to weight loss.

6. Women have several key hormones that thrive when they eat different foods. Therefore, your diet should vary based on your hormones.

Milestone Goals

1. What are some toxins you should avoid?

_____
_____
_____
_____
_____

2. Are low-fat and fat-free foods as healthy as they sound?

_____
_____
_____
_____
_____

3. What is a set point, and how does it change when you restrict calories?

_____
_____
_____
_____
_____

4. What increases cortisol?

_____
_____
_____
_____
_____

Action Plan

1. Forgive yourself for making any of the five dieting mistakes in the past.

_____
_____
_____

_____

_____

2. Commit to avoiding the five dieting mistakes in the future.

_____

_____

_____

_____

_____

3. Imagine a healthier version of yourself. What does that look like?

_____

_____

_____

_____

_____

Chapter 2: Healing Power Of Fasting

In Chapter Two, "Healing Power of Fasting," the author addresses three main points:

1. A brief history of fasting and its modern version.

2. The benefits of fasting.

3. Different types of fasting and their specific benefits.

The author recognizes that fasting is rare in modern times. However, fasting was a way of life for our prehistoric ancestors. Depending on food supplies, hunting, and gathering, it was either feast or famine. In fact, some scientists think there may still be a thrifty gene in our DNA that thrives on this feast-or-famine diet. While fasting is not as common today, Ramadan is a prime example of fasting in the modern age. Ramadan is a religious fast. However, this type of fast, like any other, can have many health benefits for participants.

The author lists many benefits of fasting. These benefits are:

- **Increased Ketones** - When our bodies can't get energy from sugar, they turn to stored fat, which they process through ketones. Another benefit of fasting is autophagy. This process literally means self-cleaning and is the process cells use to clean and repair themselves.

- **Breakdown of glycogen** - When our bodies get too much sugar, this sugar gets stored as glycogen. The most common places for bodies to store glycogen are in the muscles, liver, and fat. By fasting, our body is forced to use this glycogen for energy, improving the function of these organs.

- **Production of the growth hormone** - The growth hormone helps us stay young, build muscles, burn fat, and support the brain. While our bodies stop producing this hormone around thirty years of age, fasting can stimulate the production of this hormone again.

- **Dopamine production** - Dopamine is a feel-good hormone and can be produced whenever we eat. However, we can become addicted to increased dopamine levels and use food to literally feed this addiction. Fasting helps to reset dopamine levels and break this addiction.

- **Support the immune system** - Studies of cancer patients have shown that taking a water fast of 72 hours helps the body to clear out old white blood cells and replace them with new, healthy white blood cells.

- **Support gut health** - The author notes that there are ten times the amount of bacteria in the gut as human cells in the body. This bacteria is crucial for the digestive system to function properly. But antibiotics, stress, and certain foods can kill off this gut microbiome. Antibiotics are especially harmful as 90% of our gut biome can be killed by just one round of antibiotics. However, fasting gives your natural microbiome a chance to replenish and your GI system to function like new again.

- **Prevent recurrence of cancer -** The book cites a 2016 study published in the Journal of The American Medical Association. In this study of two thousand women who had beaten cancer, the results found a 64% reduction in the likelihood of these women developing breast cancer again after fasting for at least thirteen hours.

After addressing the benefits of fasting, the author moves on to the five types of fasting. Each type of fasting lasts for a different length and can offer unique health benefits. These five types of fasting are:

1. **Intermittent fasting** - The first fasting type lasts for only 12 to 16 hours and is known as Intermittent fasting. The author recommends people start intermittent fasting by pushing their breakfast back by just an hour every day until they are fasting for at least fourteen hours. Some of the benefits of this type of fasting include weight loss, increased brain function, and more energy.

2. **Autophagy fasting** - This type of fasting lasts for 17 to 72 hours. The longer this fast continues, the more autophagy will occur. As autophagy is the process cells use to clean up, this type of fasting helps the body remove toxins, increase memory, and boost the immune system. Another benefit of autophagy fasting is that it can help balance sex hormones, as autophagy positively affects ovaries.

3. **Gut-reset fasting** - This fasting type takes at least seventy-two hours, and the author notes that it is her favorite type of fasting. As its name suggests, this fasting type supports gut health. When you

fast for at least seventy-two hours, your gut can replenish any natural microbiomes lost due to antibiotics. Additionally, gut-reset fasting can offset the leaky gut syndrome attributed to birth control pills.

4. **Dopamine reset fasting** - To complete a dopamine reset fast, you must fast for at least forty-eight hours. Our bodies can lower their baseline dopamine levels during a fast of this length. This can positively impact mental health, and the author notes that many of her clients experience a positive mood change even weeks after completing a dopamine fast.

5. **Immune-Reset fasting** - This final type of fasting is also known as a 3-5 day water fast. This fast lasts at least 72 hours. After this point, old white blood cells begin to be replaced with new, healthy ones. The book notes that some research has been done on this fasting type. It may help reduce the risk of cancer as it gives the body a chance to clear out any cancer cells before they become a problem.

This second chapter ends with encouragement from the author that fasting is a personal exercise and women should learn about fasting to find the system that best supports them. The author promises to continue with a more thorough explanation of the considerations of fasting, like metabolic switching, unique hormone profiles, and how to vary the length of fasts.

Key Points

1. Our ancestors used to fast frequently due to the nature of their hunter-gatherer lifestyle.

2. Fasting has a host of health benefits.

3. Different fasting lengths have different health benefits.

4. Each woman should find the fasting schedule that works best for her.

Milestone Goals

1. What is a modern-day example of fasting?

_____

_____

_____

_____

_____

2. What is the benefit of fasting you want to see in your life?

_____

_____

_____

_____

_____

3. Which of the five types of fasts is most aligned with your health goals?

_____

_____

_____

_____

_____

4. How will you tailor fasts for your lifestyle and
   health goals?

_____

_____

_____

_____

_____

Action Plan

1. Begin to push your breakfast back by an hour until
   you are fasting for at least 14 hours a day.

_____

_____

_____

_____

_____

2. If you don't want to move your breakfast, you can
   begin to move your dinner up by an hour until you
   reach the fourteen-hour fasting goal.

_____

_____

_____

_____

_____

3. Decide on a health goal of your own and pick the fast that aligns with this goal.

_____
_____
_____
_____
_____

Chapter 3: Metabolic Switching

Chapter three," Metabolic Switching: The Missing Key to Weight Loss," picks up the promise at the end of Chapter Two by focusing on metabolic switching. The author notes that our bodies are virtually new every seven years, the amount of time it takes all our cells to replace themself. While this may sound like great news, the author states that sick cells will continue to replicate into more sick cells. Metabolic switching is needed to make cells healthy again.

As the book explains, metabolic switching is the process our bodies use to alternate between using glucose and ketones for fuel.

Metabolic switching is the process our bodies use to alternate between using glucose and ketones for fuel.

Recall from the previous chapters that ketones are how bodies use stored fats and sugars for energy. Our ancestors were often metabolic switching as they ate feast or famine style, depending on the prevalence of food. However, in the modern age, food is all around us. Many people never experience metabolic switching.

This is especially concerning as metabolic switching has a host of health benefits. These health benefits are:

1. Switching between autophagy and mTOR

2. Hormetic stress

3. Mitochondria healing

4. Regenerate neurons

The first benefit of metabolic switching is that it allows the brain to toggle between autophagy and mTOR. Autophagy is the process cells use to clean up, and mTOR equates to cell growth. The book states that eating too often increases mTOR levels, which in turn speed up cell growth and therefore shorten cell life. While fasting decreases these mTOR levels, fasting too much can have negative consequences like muscle breakdown. For these reasons, metabolic switching is important so the body can capitalize on both autophagy and mTOR.

The second benefit of metabolic switching the book addresses is hormetic stress. This type of stress is a low-level stress that helps make cells more adaptable. As cells become more adaptable, they also become healthier and more efficient. Our bodies can adapt to patterns, so changing fasting and diets is important to continue reaping the benefits of hormetic stress. As an example, the book highlights how weightlifters often change their routines to keep their muscles from becoming too used to a workout. Through hormetic stress, metabolic switching does the same thing to our cells.

A third benefit of metabolic switching the book addresses is how it helps the mitochondria heal. As you likely remember from science or health classes, the mitochondria are the powerhouse of the cell and are responsible for providing energy and detoxing the cells. Our heart, liver, brain, eyes, and muscles are especially rich in mitochondria. According to research conducted by Thomas Seyfried and published in cancer as a Metabolic Disease, there is evidence that cancer begins with the malfunctioning mitochondria, not genetics as previously thought. Unhealthy mitochondria prefer ketones (energy from stored fats and sugars) over glucose, as ketones help the mitochondria in two specific ways:

1. **Ketones help mitochondria produce glutathione**, a master antioxidant that helps the cell detox.

2. **Ketones help the mitochondria with the methylation process**. Through this process, toxins are pushed out of cells. Since sick mitochondria do not produce enough glutathione and do not methylate efficiently, providing ketones as fuel to the mitochondria helps this cell powerhouse heal itself.

The final benefit of metabolic switching is how it can help the brain regenerate neurons. Not receiving the right nutrition, being exposed to toxins, and not being utilized enough can all damage neutrons in the brain. This is particularly concerning as degenerating neurons can lead to Alzheimer's. However, metabolic switching helps to combat failing neurons. The author provides examples of women in their fifties feeling mentally sharper than they did in their thirties, all due to metabolic switching.

After covering the benefits of metabolic switching, the book moves on to address the specific health concerns metabolic switching can address. These health concerns are:

1. **Aging** - Metabolic switching helps make cells more adaptable, which also makes them healthier. Additionally, alternate-day fasting has been shown to increase the SIRT1 gene, a gene known for anti-aging.

2. **Weight Loss** - While fasting, the body is forced to use stored fats and sugars for food.

3. **Memory problems** - The author notes that 50% of brain cells prefer glucose, and the other half prefer energy from ketones. Metabolic switching ensures brain cells are getting energy from both of these sources.

4. **Reduced risk of cancer** - As cancer starts with dysfunctional mitochondria, fasting gives the mitochondria a chance to repair themselves. Metabolic switching also helps remove toxins from the body through autophagy. When people begin fasting, they can experience brain fog, bloating, diarrhea, constipation, and low energy as the body removes excess toxins. In chapter ten, strategies to reduce these symptoms are covered.

5. **Autoimmune conditions** - These conditions can be caused by problems in the gut, too many toxins, or genetic predispositions. Metabolic switching can improve all these causes of autoimmune conditions.

In Chapter three, metabolic switching is defined, and the benefits of metabolic switching are addressed. This chapter then addresses five specific health concerns that metabolic switching can improve. The chapter ends with the promise that now that the reader understands the science behind fasting and metabolic switching, it's time to learn how to apply these techniques in your own life based on your own hormonal needs.

Key Points

1. Our cells replace themselves every seven years. You want to ensure your cells are healthy so they can replicate into more, newer healthy cells.

2. Metabolic switching is how our bodies switch from using glucose as fuel to using ketones as fuel.

3. Metabolic switching has four key health benefits: switching between autophagy and mTOR, hormetic stress, mitochondria healing, and regenerating neurons.

4. Metabolic switching can also address such health concerns as aging, weight loss, memory issues, cancer, and autoimmune conditions.

Milestone Goals

1. What is hormetic stress?

_____
_____
_____
_____
_____

2. What two ways do ketones help the mitochondria of cells?

_____
_____
_____

_____

_____

3. How do autophagy and mTOR differ? How do these two processes work together?

_____

_____

_____

_____

_____

4. What are ketones?

_____

_____

_____

_____

_____

5. Do the cells in your brain prefer glucose or ketones for fuel?

_____

_____

_____

_____

_____

Action Plan

1. Explain the benefits of fasting in your own words.

_____

_____

_____
_____
_____

2. Explain the benefits of metabolic switching in your own words.

_____
_____
_____
_____
_____

Determine what benefits of metabolic fasting you want to see in your own life.

_____
_____
_____
_____
_____

3. See if you have any of the five health concerns that metabolic switching can address

_____
_____
_____
_____
_____

Chapter 4: Fasting a Woman's Way

In the fourth chapter, "Fasting a Woman's Way," the author opens with the story of Bridget. At forty-two, Bridget began to experience weight gain. The diet and exercises Bridget had previously used to lose weight were not working. So, Bridget began to fast. For six months, she saw great results while fasting. After six months, she began to feel anxious, have panic attacks, and lose her hair.

Bridget visited her doctor, who told Bridget to stop fasting. The doctor told Bridget that fasting was not for women. However, Bridget began to learn more about fasting and found the author's Youtube videos. Following the author's advice, Bridget could begin fasting again and experience the same health benefits with no downsides.

Bridget's success can be attributed to the information presented in this fourth chapter. In this chapter, the author has three key takeaways for readers:

1. Fasting should be tailored to your unique hormonal cycle

2. The hormonal hierarchy is essential to understanding how your hormones work together and impact your body and health

3. Women need to fast differently than men.

To properly understand how fasting should be tailored to one's hormonal cycle, the author walks readers through a typically 28-day menstrual cycle. However, the author does note that every woman will have a different cycle length. Twenty-eight days are just the most common length. Testosterone and progesterone are at their lowest on the first ten days of one's menstrual cycle. Estrogen is building in the body, peaking at day thirteen. As estrogen helps the skin, strengthens bones, and supports ligaments, the author recognizes that this period is an excellent time to complete emotionally difficult tasks.

The next phase of a twenty-eight-day cycle lasts from day ten to day fifteen and is the ovulation period. During his phase, estrogen and testosterone play a key role. Due to these hormones, many women feel empowered during this phase. For this reason, it's a great time to begin a new project, complete a difficult task, or take on a higher workload. Additionally, the presence of more testosterone helps with muscle building, so strength training is an excellent exercise during this time. During the next phase, lasting from day sixteen to eighteen, even more, testosterone is made, which can cause less energy and a fuzzier mind.

The fourth phase of the menstrual cycle lasts from day nineteen until bleeding. During this time, many women feel calmer and want a more relaxed schedule. Progesterone peaks six to eight days after ovulation and helps the uterine lining prepare for the egg. Dehydroepiandrosterone (DHEA) is the hormone needed to produce progesterone. Since DHEA is negatively impacted by cortisol, it's important to keep stress low during this phase. For this reason, the author does not recommend fasting during this stage so that cortisol doesn't spike.

After addressing the phases of the hormonal cycle, the author explains the hormonal hierarchy. In this hierarchy, the hormones progesterone, estrogen, and testosterone are controlled by insulin. In turn, insulin is linked to cortisol. When cortisol increases, so does insulin. At the top of this hierarchy is oxytocin, the feel-good hormone. In other words, the hormonal hierarchy is as follows:

1. Oxytocin

2. Cortisol

3. Insulin

4. Progesterone, Estrogen, & Testosterone

These hormones are all related because of the hypothalamus and pituitary in the brain. The hypothalamus notes the hormones in the body and tells the pituitary what other hormones should be created. Since oxytocin is at the top of the hierarchy, it is crucial to support this hormone. Oxytocin can be supported by meditating, practicing yoga, having a message, snuggling, having sex, and expressing gratitude.

The final takeaway from this chapter is why women need to fast differently than men. One reason for this is that men have only a twenty-four-hour hormonal cycle, whereas women have a (roughly) twenty-eight-day cycle. Another reason for fasting differences is due to toxic loads. Toxins are heavily impacted by hormone production. When hormones shift, toxins stored in the body can be released. In fact, the CDC notes that pregnant women release lead in their bones due to changes in hormones.

These differences are why many women have vastly different experiences fasting than men. The author closes with a story of Jude, who started fasting with her husband. Only Jude did not have the same positive experience as her husband. Instead, she gained weight and became anxious. By learning about her hormonal cycle, the hormonal hierarchy, and the fasting needs of women versus men, Jude was able to change her fasting schedule and see the same positive effects of fasting as her husband.

Key Points

1. Women have a 28-day hormonal cycle (though this varies from woman to woman), whereas men have a 24-hour cycle. Therefore, women should eat and fast differently during different phases of their cycle.

2. The four phases of a woman's cycle are days 1-10 (lowest testosterone and progesterone), days 10-15 (ovulation period), days 16-18 (testosterone peaks), and days 19- bleed (progesterone peaks).

3. There are six key hormones that interact with each other in a hormonal hierarchy. Oxytocin is the top hormone on this hierarchy.

4. Women have a different hormonal cycle than men, but they are also more susceptible to toxins. When fasting, women should take these differences into account.

Milestone Goals

1. During what phase of your cycle should you not fast? What is the reasoning for not fasting?

_____

_____

_____

_____

_____

2. How can you support oxytocin production and help your hormonal hierarchy?

_____

_____

_____

_____

_____

3. When in your cycle is it best to take on more work or start a difficult project?

_____

_____

_____

_____

_____

4. What can cause stored toxins in the body to be released?

_____

_____

_____

_____
_____

5. What hormone directly controls progesterone, testosterone, and estrogen?

_____
_____
_____
_____
_____

Action Plan

1. Be able to identify the four phases of women's hormonal cycle.

_____
_____
_____
_____
_____

2. Understand how each of the three sex hormones changes throughout one's hormonal cycle.

_____
_____
_____
_____
_____

3. Recognize the hormone hierarchy and understand that oxytocin is the key hormone.

_____

_____

_____

_____._____

_____

4. Realize that women need to fast differently than
    men because they have a different hormone cycle.

_____

_____

_____

_____

_____

Chapter 5: Build a Fasting Lifestyle Unique to You

Chapter five, "Build a Fasting Lifestyle Unique to You," begins the second part of this book. In this chapter, the author acknowledges that healthcare is often still treated as a one size fits all solution. However, there is a growing movement for personalized healthcare, also known as functional medicine. This concept of functional medicine dates back to Hippocrates. This father of medicine tailored his treatments to the age, physique, and constitution of his patients.

In modern times, functional medicine plays a role in the *n-to-1* concept. In this treatment solution, patients play a part in deciding which treatment option to pursue. The author encourages readers to take the same approach when fasting. To tailor fasting to one's specific goals, the author identifies four pillars one should consider when determining a fasting protocol:

1. Identify your fasting goals

2. Switch up your fasting lengths

3. Eat a variety of foods

4. Build a community with other fasters

The first pillar involves identifying one's goals for fasting. The author mentions three goals many people have for fasting. These goals are to lose weight, balance hormones, and alleviate a specific condition. The author notes that it can take over ninety days before fasting can balance hormones. A urinary hormone test can be helpful in understanding your specific hormone levels.

The next pillar of fasting is to vary fasting lengths. The author states that people should strive for a base fasting schedule of an eight-hour eating window. However, to avoid plateaus and encourage progress, longer fasts are needed. When scheduling these longer fasts, it's important to consider the natural hormonal cycle. Fasting should also be varied based on one's social life, vacations, holidays, and other commitments.

The third pillar of fasting is to vary food choices. According to the author, many women only eat the same thirty foods. However, variety is crucial for maintaining gut health and balancing hormones. In fact, gut bacteria have an impact on cravings. When only certain foods are eaten, particular gut bacteria are allowed to flourish and can trigger cravings. By varying one's diet, a wider variety of gut bacteria can grow, thereby reducing cravings.

The fourth and final fasting pillar is to surround yourself with a community of support. The author encourages readers to find a group of women to fast with, exercise with, and encourage. Additionally, this support network can build strong relationships, increasing oxytocin in the brain and helping to balance sex hormones.

After addressing these four pillars of fasting considerations, the author recognizes three lifestyle considerations that should be analyzed when deciding how to fast. One's relationship, schedule, and activity level should all impact how a woman fasts.

Chapter four ends with an encouraging reminder that women should not compare their fasting schedule and results to the men in their life. Instead, fasting should be tailored to each individual woman. Additionally, the author encourages women to see failure as a chance to learn, grow, and adapt rather than be discouraged.

Key Points

1. Personalized healthcare is the idea that medicine and health initiatives should be tailored to the individual. This holds true for fasting.

2. When fasting, you should have a goal in mind. Common goals are to lose weight, balance hormones, or alleviate a specific condition.

3. You should vary the length of your fasts based on your hormones, social life, and health goals.

4. You should eat a variety of food to support your gut and hormones.

5. Community is essential when fasting as the community provides a support network and can increase oxytocin.

Milestone Goals

1. What is your personal health goal for fasting?

_____

_____

_____

_____
_____

2. Why is it important to vary the length of your fasts?

_____
_____
_____
_____
_____

3. How many different foods do you think you eat in a month? How could you incorporate more healthy foods into your diet?

_____
_____
_____
_____
_____

4. Do you know other women who fast? If not, how could you build a community with other women who fast?

_____
_____
_____
_____
_____

Action Plan

1. Pick a reason to begin fasting.

_____
_____
_____
_____
_____

2. Begin to fast for sixteen hours a day, but adjust based on your hormonal cycle.

_____
_____
_____
_____
_____

3. Add a wider variety of foods to your daily diet.

_____
_____
_____
_____
_____

4. Build a network of other women committed to fasting so you can support each other.

_____
_____
_____
_____
_____

Chapter 6: Foods That Support Your Hormones

Chapter 6, "Foods that Support Your Hormones," introduces four food principles. These principles are:

1. The Ingredients in your food

2. The glycemic load of your food

3. Eat a variety of foods

4. Vary your diet according to your menstrual cycle

The first principle, ingredients matter, can be summarized by reading your ingredient labels. When reading labels, it's important to check the number of ingredients (ideally less than five) and spend extra time analyzing the first five ingredients. You should also check the ingredient labels to identify any toxins, as well as the types of oils, sugars, and flours. Lastly, you should check that there are no artificial colors or flavors.

When it comes to ingredients, there are certain ones that can support hormones, muscle building, and gut biome. Good fats, seeds, nuts, legumes, fruits, and vegetables all support estrogen. Progesterone thrives when you eat root and cruciferous vegetables, tropical and citrus fruits, as well as seeds and legumes. For building muscle, you want to focus on proteins rich in leucine, isoleucine, and valine amino acids. Chicken, beef, pork, fish, milk, cheese, eggs, tofu, and navy beans are all good choices. To support your gut biome, the author recommends probiotic, prebiotic, and polyphenol foods. Probiotic foods are often fermented and include sauerkraut, kimchi, pickles, yogurt, and kefir. Good sources of prebiotics include onions, garlic, leeks, asparagus, hummus, chickpeas, and cashews. Lastly, polyphenol foods are rich in antioxidants and include foods like artichokes, brussels sprouts, rosemary, thyme, basil, dark chocolate, and red wine.

The next principle of healthy eating the book addresses is glycemic load. A glycemic load is a number from 1-100. Foods close to 100 cause a higher spike in blood sugar. The author recommends understanding macronutrients or macros to keep your blood sugar in check so you can select foods with a lower glycemic index. There are three types of macros, carbohydrates, protein, and fats.

1. **Carbohydrates** can be classified into two types, simple and complex. To easily differentiate between the two, simple carbohydrates are man-made and can be seen in processed foods. Complex carbohydrates are nature-made and include fruits and vegetables. Of the two, complex carbohydrates are the healthier option and have a lower glycemic index.

2. **Protein** is the next type of macronutrient. This macro impacts blood sugar in three ways. First, protein breaks down into glucose much slower than carbohydrates. Secondly, protein is absorbed much slower than carbs. Lastly, protein helps you feel full for longer.

3. **Fat** is the final macronutrient. Fat comes in two types, good fats, and bad fats. Good fats are the ones that provide valuable nutrients for cells, whereas bad fats inflame cells. Good fats have the

additional benefit of stabilizing blood sugar and reducing hunger.

The third principle of healthy eating is the importance of a diverse diet. The author recommends eating at least two hundred different types of foods over the span of a month. In order to qualify, food must be a complex card, protein, or fat. However, spices do count towards diverse eating and are an excellent way to add more variety to your diet. Some spices the author recommends are cardamom, cumin, star anise, turmeric, black pepper, cinnamon, and mustard seed.

The fourth and final principle of healthy eating this book addresses is the importance of cycling. When you are in the first part of your menstrual cycle, the author recommends a ketobiotic diet. One week before your period starts, the author suggests switching to a hormone-feasting diet. The hallmarks of a ketobiotic diet, a term the author coined, include less than 50 grams of net carbs with a focus on carbs from vegetables and greens. During a ketobiotic diet, you should also get 60% of your food with good fat and no more than 75 grams of protein. When hormone feasting, you should get 150 net carbs, with a focus on root vegetables and fruits. Protein should be no more than 50 grams, and you can eat as much healthy fat as you want.

Chapter six ends with a taste of what's to come in chapter seven. The author introduces the topic of the fasting cycle, which will be explained in the next chapter, and builds on the four food principles of chapter six.

Key Points

1. Food supports your hormones. When grocery shopping, it's important to check the ingredient labels on your food.

2. The glycemic index of a food tells you how much the food will spike your blood sugar and how much the food will help you feel full.

3. You should eat a variety of complex carbs, good fats, and healthy proteins.

4. The ketobiotic diet and hormone-feasting diet are the two diet types you should follow. The specific diet you should follow will vary with your menstrual cycle.

Milestone Goals

1. What should you look for when reading the ingredients label on food?

_____

_____

_____

_____

_____

2. Are foods with a lower or higher glycemic index better for you?

_____

_____

_____

_____

_____

3. What are the three different macronutrients?

_____

_____

_____

_____

_____

4. What are some spices you can add to your diet to increase the variety of foods you eat?

_____

_____

_____

_____

_____

5. How many carbs should you eat on the ketobiotic diet? What about the hormone-feasting diet?

_____

_____

_____

_____

_____

Action Plan

1. Begin checking the ingredients of all foods you purchase

_____

_____

_____

_____

_____

2. Eat foods with a low glycemic load.

_____

_____

_____

_____

_____

3. Strive to eat at least 200 different types of foods in a month.

_____

_____

_____

_____

_____

4. Understand the ketobiotic and hormone-feasting diets so you can apply them to your life after reading the next chapter.

_____

_____

_____

_____

_____

Chapter 7: The Fasting Cycle

The seventh chapter of the book, "The Fasting Cycle," begins with the reminder that women should fast differently than men. This is due to women's natural hormonal cycle. To work with this natural cycle, the author recommends using the Fasting Cycle to reap the benefits of fasting and honor one's natural hormonal cycle.

The fasting cycle has three separate phases:

1. Power phase

2. Manifestation phase

3. Nurture phase

In the book, these phases are built around a thirty-day cycle. However, the author encourages readers to adapt this fasting cycle to their hormonal cycle. For cycles less than thirty days, continue following the last phase of the cycle until your next period starts. For cycles shorter than thirty days, start at day one whenever your period begins. For women who do not have a period or are postmenopausal, the author promises to detail a reset that these women should follow in the next chapter.

The first phase of the fasting cycle is the power phase. This phase occurs on days one through ten and again on days sixteen through nineteen of a thirty-day cycle. During this phase, one should fast for thirteen to seventy-two hours. Longer fasts are especially important during days sixteen through nineteen as sex hormones are at their lowest, so autophagy is especially helpful for cell healing. Diet during this phase should be ketobiotic to focus on autophagy and ketosis. This diet also helps to keep glucose and insulin low during this period to lower insulin and support estrogen.

The second fasting phase is the manifestation phase, which occurs during ovulation. For a thirty-day cycle, ovulation occurs during days eleven through fifteen. During this phase, the book recommends fasting for thirteen to sixteen hours and eating a hormone-feasting diet. The hormones estrogen and testosterone are at their peak during this phase, which helps one feel strong and powerful. For this reason, completing more strenuous workouts or starting difficult work projects during this time can boost your success.

The final phase of the fasting cycle is the nurture phase. This phase begins on day twenty of a thirty-day cycle and ends with the first day of a woman's period. Fasting is not recommended during this phase. Instead, following a hormone-feasting diet is important so progesterone can get the carbohydrates it loves. However, the author states that complex carbs, rather than simple ones, are the better option. The author also recommends keeping stress low during this phase as progesterone, the primary hormone in the nurture phase is negatively impacted by cortisol.

The author closes this seventh chapter with the hope that women feel encouraged to start fasting after learning about the fasting cycle. The author also introduces the thirty-day fasting reset, a specific diet for fasting women, which will be covered in full in the next chapter.

Key Points

1. The fasting cycle is a fasting schedule created by the author to help women fast and eat in accordance with their natural cycle.

2. The first phase of the fasting cycle is the power phase. This phase occurs on days 1-10 of a 30-day cycle. During this time, you should fast for 13-72 hours and eat a ketobiotic diet.

3. The manifestation phase occurs on days 11-15. Fasts during this time are 13 - 16 hours, and you should eat a hormone-feasting diet.

4. On days 16 - 19, you are in the power phase again. Like the first power phase, fast for 13-72 hours and eat a ketobiotic diet.

5. The final phase is the nurture phase. This phase ends on the first day of your period. During this time, don't fast and eat a hormone-feasting diet.

Milestone Goals

1. What are the three phases of the fasting cycle?

_____
_____
_____
_____
_____

2. What should you eat during the power phase?

_____
_____

_____

_____

_____

3. Should you fast during the nurture phase?

_____

_____

_____

_____

_____

4. How long should you fast during the manifestation phase?

_____

_____

_____

_____

_____

Action Plan

1. Identify which phase of your hormonal cycle you are in.

_____

_____

_____

_____

_____

2. Begin to follow the appropriate diet and fasting protocol for the fasting phase you are currently in

_____

_____

_____

_____

_____

3. When hormone feasting, strive to eat complex carbs rather than simple carbs.

_____

_____

_____

_____

_____

4. Keep your stress levels low during your nurture phase.

_____

_____

_____

_____

_____

Chapter 8: 30-Day Fasting Reset

Chapter eight, "30-Day Fasting Reset", introduces a thirty-day plan to help readers get started on their fasting journey. Before starting this fasting reset, the author encourages readers to track their menstrual cycle (if they have a period). The author then recommends timing the reset to your menstrual cycle. This means if your menstrual cycle is only twenty-eight days, the reset should be that long as well. Additionally, the author recognizes that the reset includes fasts of thirteen to twenty hours, which can be difficult. To overcome these difficulties, the author recommends readers have an action plan in place when difficulties arise.

Another suggestion the author has for fasters is to join a community of other fasters. The author cites a study Harvard conducted from 1938 to 2018. This study found a positive correlation between supportive relationships and health. For readers who don't know other women who fast, the author states that she has several free online communities readers can join.

The book explains that this thirty-day fasting reset is designed for any woman, whether or not they have a cycle. Some health concerns this fast can address include weight-loss resistance, insulin resistance, memory problems, menopause symptoms, low energy, hair loss, and digestive issues. However, the author does recommend speaking to your doctor before starting any diet or fasting changes.

Before beginning the thirty-day reset fast, the book details a two-week pre-reset reader should follow. This reset includes three criteria:

1. Foods to avoid

2. Foods to add

3. Compressing your eating window

When planning meals during this pre-reset, the foods to avoid are bad oils, sugars, refined flour, and toxins. Bad oils included partially hydrogenated oils, cottonseed oil, corn oil, and vegetable oil. Sugars and flour should be avoided because of their effect on blood sugar and poor glycemic index, respectively. Lastly, toxins you should look out for include artificial colors, artificial flavorings, dyes, Splenda, and NutraSweet.

In addition to foods you should avoid during this two-week pre-reset, there are several foods you should add to your diet. These foods include good fats and healthy proteins. Some examples of good fats included in the book are olive oil, avocado oil, MCT oils, grass-fed butter, and nut butter. The book encourages readers to add these fats to their diet as they help to reduce cravings. Examples of healthy proteins that should be added to your diet include grass-fed beef, bison, turkey, chicken, pork, eggs, and charcuterie meats.

The final criterion of the two-week pre-reset is to begin compressing your eating window. This eating window is the time between your first and last meal of the day. The author suggests a thirteen-hour eating window as a goal for readers. The book has two strategies to reach this goal.

The first strategy includes pushing back breakfast by one hour every two days until the goal eating window is reached. The second strategy has readers push breakfast up by one hour and dinner back by one hour until the thirteen-hour eating window is reached. To help readers reach this goal, the author recommends drinking coffee or tea with MCT oil and cream to reduce hunger in the morning.

After completing the two-week pre-reset, it is time to begin the thirty-day fasting reset. The fasting reset is composed of four phases: Power Phase I, Manifestation Phase, Power Phase II, and Nurture Phase.

1. **Power Phase I** begins on day one and ends on day ten. During this time, you'll follow a ketobiotic diet. On the first four days, you should fast for thirteen hours. The fifth day includes a longer fast of fifteen hours, followed by seventeen-hour fasts on days six through ten.

2. **The Manifestation Phase** comes next on days eleven through fifteen. Diet in this phase should be hormone feasting, and fasts should last thirteen hours. After the Manifestation Phase is complete, a second power phase begins.

3. **Power Phase II** lasts from days sixteen through nineteen; the diet you should follow during this phase is ketobiotic. Fast lengths during this time are fifteen hours.

4. **The Nurture Phase** is the final phase of the thirty-day reset. This phase lasts from day twenty to day

thirty and utilizes a hormone-feasting diet. During this time, you should not fast.

The author designed the thirty-day reset for beginning fasters. For experienced fasters, the author includes a more advanced thirty-day reset for these readers to follow. This more advanced reset includes the same four phases as the basic reset, but fast lengths are slightly longer. For example, during Power Phase I, fasts should be fifteen, twenty-four, and seventeen hours, respectively. The Manifestation phase should include fasts of fifteen hours. During Power Phase II, you should start with a twenty-four-hour fast, then follow seventeen-hour fasts for the rest of the phase. During the final Nurture Phase, the book recommends fasting for thirteen hours.

Whether you choose the basic or more advanced thirty-day fasting reset, the author recommends some tools to help readers during this reset. These tools are known as biometrics and include monitoring blood sugar and ketones. However, the author states that using these tools during the thirty-day reset is not required. If a reader chooses to use them, the author recommends taking your blood sugar three times daily and your ketone levels twice daily. The first measurement should be in the morning, right after waking up. The second measurement should be right before eating your first meal of the day. The author states that the second reading should ideally have lower blood sugar and higher ketones. This means your body is effectively switching from burning food to burning stored fats and sugars. The third and final reading of the day should be two hours after eating and should only measure blood sugar. Ideally, blood sugar levels between the second and third readings should be relatively the same. This means you are insulin sensitive.

The author ends the chapter with a reminder that readers should enjoy the fasting process. Additionally, while challenges will arise, having a community to help support you is key to fasting success.

Key Points

1. Before starting a fasting practice in your own life, complete the author's two-week pre-fasting reset to make fasting easier.

2. During the fasting reset, try to limit bad oils, sugars, flours, and toxins from your diet.

3. During the fasting reset, add good fats and healthy proteins into your diet.

4. Compress your eating window to a thirteen-hour period.

5. After the two-week fasting reset, you are ready to begin the fasting cycle.

Milestone Goals

1. Based on your social life and calendar, when would be a good time for you to start the two-week pre-reset?

_____

_____

_____

_____

_____

2. What are some toxins you should remove from
   your diet?

_____

_____

_____

_____

_____

3. What good fats and healthy proteins should you
   add to your diet?

_____

_____

_____

_____

_____

4. What is your current eating window (time between
   your first and last meal)? How long should this
   eating window be?

_____

_____

_____

_____

_____

5. Do you have a blood sugar monitor and ketone
   monitor to help your fasts? If not, do you plan on
   getting one?

_____
_____
_____
_____
_____

Action Plan

1. Begin tracking your menstrual cycle if you have one.

_____
_____
_____
_____
_____

2. Remove the foods to avoid from your diet and begin incorporating healthy proteins and good fats.

_____
_____
_____
_____
_____

3. Move our breakfast back by an hour until you've reached a thirteen-hour fasting window.

_____
_____
_____
_____
_____

4. Look at your calendar and pick a time to start the thirty-day fasting reset.

_____

_____

_____

_____

_____

5. Decide if you want to follow the basic or advanced fasting reset.

_____

_____

_____

_____

_____

Chapter 9: How to Break a Fast

In the ninth chapter of the book, "How to Break a Fast," the author covers just that - how to break a fast. When breaking a fast, the author notes that very little research has been done regarding the best foods to eat. The author explains that she has tested several ways of ending a fast and found four of the most common fast-breaking strategies. These strategies are:

1. Fast-breaking foods to help reset the gut's microbiome

2. Fast-breaking foods to help build muscle

3. Fast-breaking foods to burn fat

4. Eating whatever sounds good to you

The first fast-breaking strategy is best for those who want to reset their microbiome. The author recommends eating foods high in probiotics, prebiotics, and polyphenols. In this section, the author describes her favorite fast-breaking meal for gut health: one half an avocado with one cup of sauerkraut and a sprinkling of pumpkin seeds and flaxseed oil. Other foods the author recommends include fermented yogurts, bone broth, kombucha, seeds, and seed oils.

The next fast-breaking method is designed for people who are trying to build muscle. The author addresses a common misconception that fasting makes muscles smaller. However, the author assures readers that this is not the case. Muscles just appear smaller after a fast because sugar in the muscles has been released through the fasting process. It is paramount to eat a meal with protein to maintain and build muscle after a fast. Some protein options included in the book are eggs, beef sticks/jerky, chicken breast, and protein shakes made from peas, hemp, or whey.

The third fasting technique is best for those who are trying to burn fat. The author reminds readers that fats help to stabilize blood sugar, so ending a fast with fat is a good way to extend this benefit. However, the book notes that not all fats will break a fast for every person. Depending on your microbiome diversity and insulin resistance, you may find some fats will break or fast while others will not. To test whether fat breaks your fast, the author recommends taking your blood pressure before eating or drinking the food in question and then again thirty minutes later. If your blood sugar is consistent between these measurements, this fat did not break your fast.

Some common fats that don't break a fast are supplements and medication, black coffee and coffee with full-fat cream, teas, flaxseed oil, MCT oil, mineral water, and small amounts of nut butter. However, the author recommends testing these fats for yourself before consuming them while fasting.

The final fast-breaking strategy involves eating whatever tastes best to you. The author does caution readers against this strategy. While eating whatever tests best does provide instant satisfaction, it limits the healing effect of the fast. To reap the full rewards of a fast, the author suggests following another fast-breaking strategy.

For fasts longer than forty-eight hours, the author includes a four-step eating plan to end the fast.

1. Sip a cup of bone broth.

2. Wait an hour, then eat a meal full of probiotics and good fat.

3. After waiting another hour, eat some steamed vegetables. If you feel bloated after this meal, it is likely due to gut issues. If this is the case for you, the author recommends following the advice in the book to improve your gut microbiome.

4. Eat a meal with plenty of animal protein, at least thirty grams.

No matter how you choose to end a fast, the author closes this chapter with the reminder that better food choices after a fast will equate to more health benefits and faster progress toward your health goals.

Key Points

1. You should break a fast with food that supports your health goals.

2. If you want to improve your gut health, break your fast with foods rich in polyphenols, probiotics, and prebiotics.

3. If you want to build muscle, break your fast with a protein-rich meal.

4. If you want to burn fat, it's important to remember that not every fat you eat will break your fast. Use a blood sugar monitor to determine which fats will break your fast.

5. Breaking your fast with whatever tastes best can limit the health benefits of fasting and is not recommended.

Milestone Goals

1. What goals do you have for fasting?

_____

_____

_____

_____

_____

2. Based on your health goals, what should you eat to break a fast?

_____

_____

_____

_____

_____

3. Does eating full-fat cream, nut butter, and other fats always break a fast?

_____

_____

_____

_____

_____

4. How should you break a 48-hour fast?

_____

_____

_____

_____

_____

Action Plan

1. Test your blood sugar before and after eating some
    of the good fats listed in this chapter to see if it
    impacts your blood sugar.

    _____

    _____

    _____

    _____

    _____

2. Create a plan to break your fast, tailoring it to your
    health goals.

    _____

    _____

    _____

    _____

    _____

3. If you want to build muscle, plan a meal full of
    protein to break your fast.

    _____

    _____

    _____

_____

_____

4. If you want to improve your gut health, plan a meal full of probiotics, prebiotics, and polyphenols to break your fast.

_____

_____

_____

_____

_____

Chapter 10: Hacks that Make Fasting Effortless

In the tenth chapter of this book, the author covers a myriad of hacks to make fasting easier for readers. The chapter, titled "Hacks that Make Fasting Effortless," begins with a reminder that becoming healthier can be a time-consuming process. The author also recommends that readers should approach fasting as a practice. That you should celebrate your wins, and any fasting length is better than no fast at all. The author also reminds readers to approach fasting with curiosity and to think of failures only as learning activities. The hacks included in this chapter are:

1. **Identify the difference between hunger and boredom**. Suppose you want to eat to beat boredom (rather than stop hunger). In that case, the author recommends distracting yourself or finding another way to boost dopamine, like dancing or calling a friend. The author recommends a mineral pack if you are truly hungry rather than bored and don't want to end your fast yet. The author states LMNT and Redmond are her favorite mineral packs. Other ways of beating hunger include a fasting snack, like MCT oil or cream in coffee or tea. A drink with prebiotic powder added can placate your gut microbiome and help minimize your hunger.

2. **Reduce effects of toxin removal**. When fasting, your body will remove toxins from your system. The book notes that toxin removal can have similar symptoms to the flu. To prevent these feelings, the

book lists dry brushing, sweating, lymph massages, and Epsom salt baths as ways to help your body detox. Jumping on a trampoline can also help with the detoxification process, as this helps your lymphatic system. Lastly, consuming binders like zeolite or activated charcoal helps your body remove toxins so you don't experience flu-like symptoms.

3. **Use biometrics**. Another hack included in this chapter is to measure your blood sugar and ketones. The author encourages readers to follow the protocol laid out in the previous chapter if they choose to take these measurements. For people who need help decreasing their blood sugar and burning ketones during a fast, the author suggests completing longer fasts, varying fast lengths, and avoiding processed foods. Assisting your liver function by using castor oil packs, coffee enemas, infrared saunas, essential oils, bitter lettuce, and dandelion teas are other ways to decrease blood sugar and encourage ketosis. Lastly, using a DUTCH hormone test or supplements to support your adrenals and remove toxins from your life can also help lower blood sugar and help you burn ketones.

4. **Detox more effectively**. To help your body detox more effectively, the author lists sweating, drinking plenty of water, dry brushing, and massaging as helpful hacks to help drain the lymphatic system. The author notes that some women may experience missing or skipped periods as they detox. If this happens to you, the author

recommends continuing the thirty-day reset fast, as everybody detoxes differently.

The remaining hacks in this chapter are tailored to specific health concerns. The book recommends varying your fasting lengths and adding supplements if you lose hair during a fast. Suppose you experience fatigue while fasting. Red light therapy and hyperbaric chambers can reduce fatigue by supporting your mitochondria. For readers taking medication, it's best to take your medication during your eating window, but be sure to talk to your doctor about any changes to your diet, like fasting. Unlike medication, supplements can be taken anytime but should be stopped during a three-day water fast.

For readers who experience cravings, the book states that "bad" bacteria in your gut are likely causing the cravings. Continuing your fast and fasting for longer can help kill these bad bacteria and help your good bacteria flourish. Some fasters experience changes in sleep. The author notes that you may need less sleep when fasting, which is a common occurrence. However, if you have discomfort while sleeping, taking a magnesium supplement or using CBD lotions and tinctures can ease the discomfort.

For women recovering from a hysterectomy, the book suggests following the thirty-day fasting reset to balance hormones. If you have a thyroid condition, the author debunks the theory that fasting lowers thyroid hormones. Instead, the author notes that the T3 hormone will lower during a fast but returns to normal after eating. For those with adrenal fatigue, fasting can provide relief by stabilizing blood sugar.

The book does not recommend fasting for pregnant women. This is due to the fact that fasting releases toxins and you do not want these toxins to go toward your baby. Fasts while breastfeeding should be limited to thirteen hours to limit toxins. Still, the book encourages readers to talk to their doctor. For readers with diabetes or an eating disorder, the author recommends readers talk to their doctor. While fasting can benefit people with diabetes or those who are recovered from an eating disorder, talking to your doctor will ensure you fast safely.

After covering the hacks in this chapter, the author encourages readers to find one of her communities to join. The author has free Facebook groups, online communities, and a YouTube channel to help readers find other women passionate about fasting, learn more about fasting, and ask any additional questions.

Key Points

1. When fasting, be able to tell the difference between boredom and hunger.

2. Use dry brushing, Epsom salt baths, lymph massages, and jumping on a trampoline to reduce the symptoms of detoxing.

3. Use blood sugar and ketone monitors to tailor your fasts to your body.

4. If you skip a period while fasting, it is likely due to your body detoxing. Continue the fasting process and use hacks to reduce detoxing symptoms.

Milestone Goals

1. While fasting, have you experienced any negative symptoms?

   _____
   _____
   _____
   _____
   _____

2. Do you have any specific conditions that fasting could address? If so, what examples does the author provide on how fasting helps your condition?

   _____
   _____
   _____
   _____
   _____

3. How can you improve your liver function and help your body detox?

   _____
   _____
   _____
   _____
   _____

4. What are some ways to minimize hunger while fasting?

_____

_____

_____

_____

_____

Action Plan

1. Whenever you feel hungry during a fast, ask yourself if you are hungry or bored.

_____

_____

_____

_____

_____

2. Pick one (or more) of the hacks for improving your body's detoxification and work it into your daily/weekly schedule.

_____

_____

_____

_____

_____

3. As you fast, note any health concerns and use the appropriate hack in the book to address these concerns.

_____

_____

_____

_____

_____

4. If you are pregnant, breastfeeding, have diabetes, recovered from an eating disorder, or have any concerns about fasting, talk to your doctor.

_____

_____

_____

_____

_____

Chapter 11: Recipes

The final and eleventh chapter of the book is dedicated to Recipes. The author begins the chapter with a reminder for readers to eat a variety of foods and try new foods. The recipes in this chapter are divided into three sections, ketobiotic, hormone feasting, and breaking your fast. Recipes in the ketobiotic section included loaded hummus bowls, shakshuka with pickled onions and avocado, kimchi salad topped with crisped chickpeas, and a frittata with prosciutto, spinach, and asparagus. In the hormone feasting section, there are recipes to make white bean and kale soups, herby steaks with a side of mashed potatoes and vegetables, sweet potatoes stuffed with chipotle black beans, hash browns made from sweet potatoes, and quinoa tabouli, among others. The final section has recipes designed to help you break a fast and has tasty meals like a smoothie made with avocado and berries, burger patties with guacamole, avocado topped with tuna salad, a strawberry and mint flavored kefir smoothie, and a vanilla chia pudding topped with chocolate and berries.

Afterward & Appendices

The book ends with an afterword from the author. The author begins with the story of Lana, who was diagnosed with metastatic breast cancer and given three months to live. Lana beat the odds and lived another eleven years, mainly by changing her lifestyle. The author continues with her passion for fasting and excitement at seeing women make healthy changes during the COVID-19 pandemic. The book ends with the author's wish to see more women becoming empowered about their health and embracing the fasting lifestyle.

The final pages of the book are dedicated to three appendices. Appendix A is a glossary of the most often-used fasting terms. Appendix B contains a list of foods, such as probiotic-rich foods, good fats, and healthy proteins. The final appendices, Appendix C, details specific fasting protocols for specific health concerns like infertility, chronic fatigue, depression, and type II diabetes.

Background Information about *Fast Like a Girl*

Fast Like a Girl by Dr. Mindy Pelz was published in December of 2022. The book is divided into three parts. In the first part, the author details the three key hormones women have, estrogen, progesterone, and testosterone. This section also discusses how these hormones vary during a menstrual cycle and the impact of these hormones. The next section of the book deals with food and fasting. In this section, the reader learns how to tailor one's diet to your menstrual cycle and how to vary foods for increased health. The final section builds on the previous two and contains specific fasting plans laid out in an easy-to-follow manner. However, due to the uniqueness of each body, the final section includes a variety of fasting tweaks and changes so readers can tailor their fasts based on health goals and concerns.

Ultimately, the author wants readers to understand three basic concepts after reading the book. First, how long to fast? Secondly, should you eat while fasting? And lastly, why do women need to fast differently than men?

Background Information about Dr. Mindy Pelz

Dr. Mindy Pelz, the author of *Fast Like a Girl*, has dedicated her career to helping women become healthier. To educate women about their health, Dr. Pelz has a YouTube channel, podcast, and several books and has appeared on TV shows. Dr. Pelz's YouTube channel is dedicated to alternative health methods backed by science. Her channel has accumulated over 24 million lifetime views. Her podcast, the Resetter Podcast, is considered one of the top podcasts for science and nutrition.

Along with *Fast Like a Girl*, Dr. Pelz has written three other books. These are entitled *The Menopause Reset*, *The Reset Factor*, and *The Reset Factor Kitchen*. In addition to these publications, Dr. Pelz has also appeared on such shows as Extra TV and The Doctors.

Dr. Pelz also has a website to help empower women to embrace a healthier lifestyle. This website has a variety of paid programs, free resources, and products to help women make the healthiest choice for their life. Today, Dr. Pelz continues her mission to educate and empower women about their health through speaking engagements, her books, and her courses.

Discussion Questions

1. Has the author convinced you to try fasting?

2. Have you ever fasted before? If so, how long did you fast for, and what was your fasting schedule? Did you try to fast like a man, following the same schedule every day?

3. What health improvements do you hope to see in your life by fasting?

4. Now that you know how your hormones change during your cycle, will you schedule your work and life differently to align with these changes?

5. What was the most surprising thing you learned from this book?

6. Do you disagree with the author about anything? If so, what is it and why?

7. What is your plan for handling difficulties when fasting?

8. How will you build a community of women to fast with?

9. What lifestyle changes are you most excited about after reading this book?

10. Are you looking forward to metabiotic or hormone-feasting meals more?

11. What is the hormonal hierarchy? What is the key hormone of this hierarchy?

12. What are the four phases of the thirty-day fasting reset?

13. What foods do you plan on eating to end a fast?

14. Did the book convince you to remove some toxins from your life? If so, how do you plan on removing these toxins?

15. Do you think you can eat two hundred unique foods in a month? If so, why or why not?

Putting it into Practice

A Step-by-step guide for implementing the lessons introduced in this book

1. Stop making the five diet mistakes listed in Chapter 1.

2. Understand how your hormones change throughout your cycle and how these hormones impact your body. See chapters 2 and 4 if you need to review them.

3. Be able to explain what metabolic switching is and why it is so important for women. Refer to Chapter 3 if you need a refresher.

4. Before beginning any diet or lifestyle changes, it is recommended to consult with your doctor.

5. Remove toxins, bad oils, sugars, flour, and simple carbs from your diet whenever possible. These foods are detailed in Chapter Six.

6. Begin incorporating a wider variety of foods into your diet. Be sure to focus on fruits, vegetables, complex carbs, good fats, and healthy proteins. Chapter Six has examples of these healthful foods.

7. If you have a period, begin tracking your cycle.

8. Complete the two-week pre-fasting reset detailed in chapter seven.

9. Begin the thirty-day fasting reset. If you have a period, schedule this reset to your cycle. You can review Chapter 8 if you need a refresher.

10. Find the best foods for you to end a fast with. Remember that these foods should be chosen based on your health goals. A full list of these foods can be found in Chapter nine.

11. If you experience difficulties or have specific conditions, incorporate the fasting hacks in chapter ten.

More books from Smart Reads

Thank You

Hope you've enjoyed your reading experience.

We here at Smart Reads will always strive to deliver to you the highest quality guides.

So I'd like to thank you for supporting us and reading until the very end.

Before you go, would you mind leaving us a review on Amazon?

It will mean a lot to us and support us creating high quality guides for you in the future.

Thanks once again!

Warmly yours,

The Smart Reads Team

Download Your Free Gift

As a way to say "Thank You" for being a fan of our series,
I've included a free gift for you:

Brain Health: How to Nurture and Nourish Your Brain For
Top Performance

Go to www.smart-reads.com to get your
FREE book.

The Smart Reads Team

Made in the USA
Las Vegas, NV
01 August 2023

75504974R00048